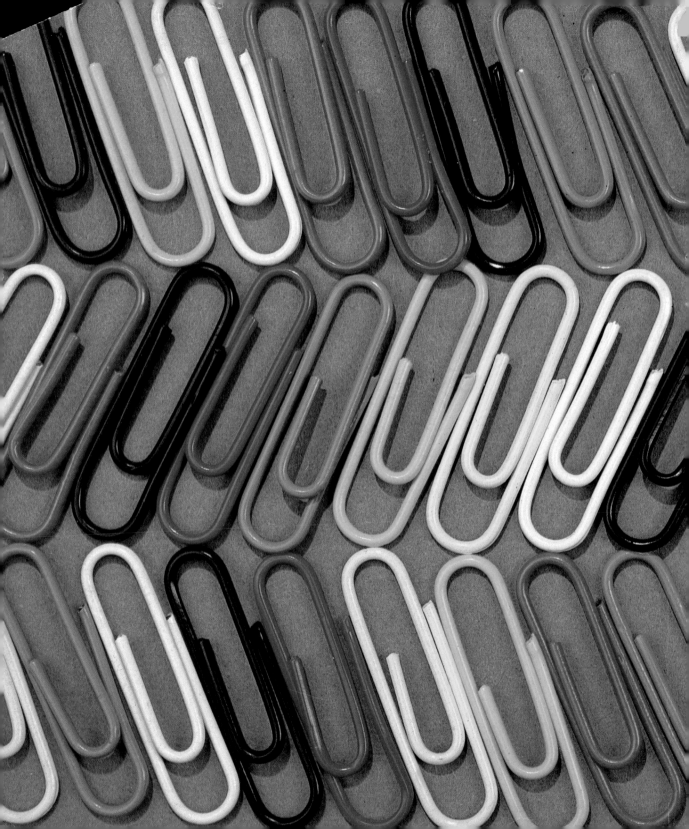

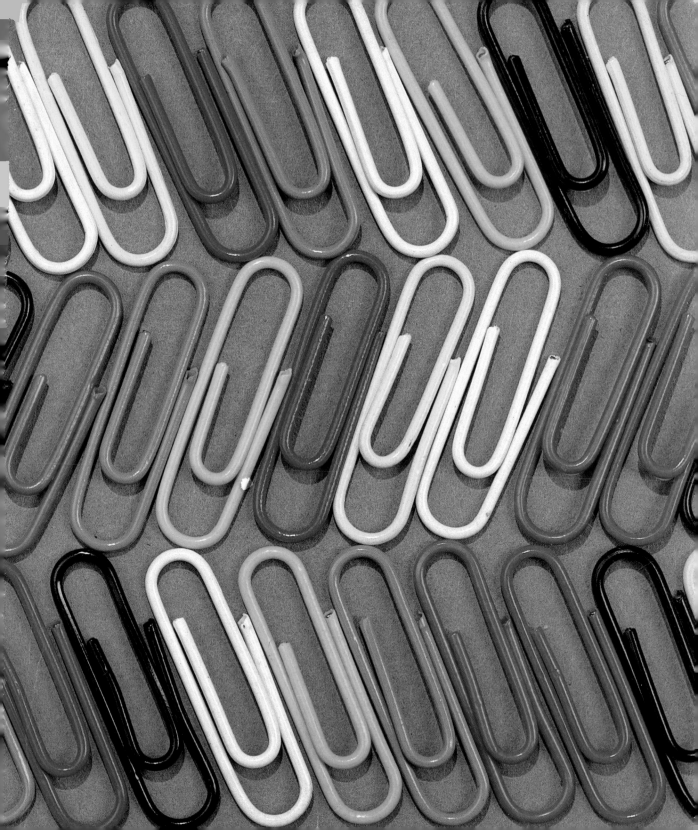

Franklin Watts Inc.
387 Park Avenue South
New York, N.Y. 10016

Library of Congress Cataloging-in-Publication Data
Pluckrose, Henry Arthur.
    Join It! / by Henry Pluckrose.
        p.    cm. — (Ways to)
    Includes index.
    Summary: Color photos and simple text explain different ways of
saying "Join it."
    ISBN 0-531-10730-2
    1. Vocabulary—Juvenile literature.   [1. Vocabulary.]   I. Title.
II. Series: Pluckrose, Henry Arthur, Ways to saying.
PE1449.P57   1989
428.1—dc20                                         89-5822
                                                      CIP
                                                      AC
© Franklin Watts 1989

Editor: Ruth Thomson
Design: K & Co

Typeset in England
by Lineage, Watford
Printed in Italy by
G. Canale S.p.A., Turin

# Ways to....
# JOIN *it!*

## Henry Pluckrose

### Photography by Chris Fairclough

**FRANKLIN WATTS**
London • New York • Sydney • Toronto

**Think how many ways there are of joining things together.**

You can hammer
in a nail to fix
wood together...

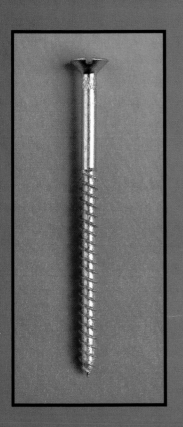

**or use a screwdriver and a screw. A screw is stronger than a nail. The pattern along its edge bites into the wood.**

Nails and screws
join pieces of
wood, but we
wouldn't use them
to join paper.

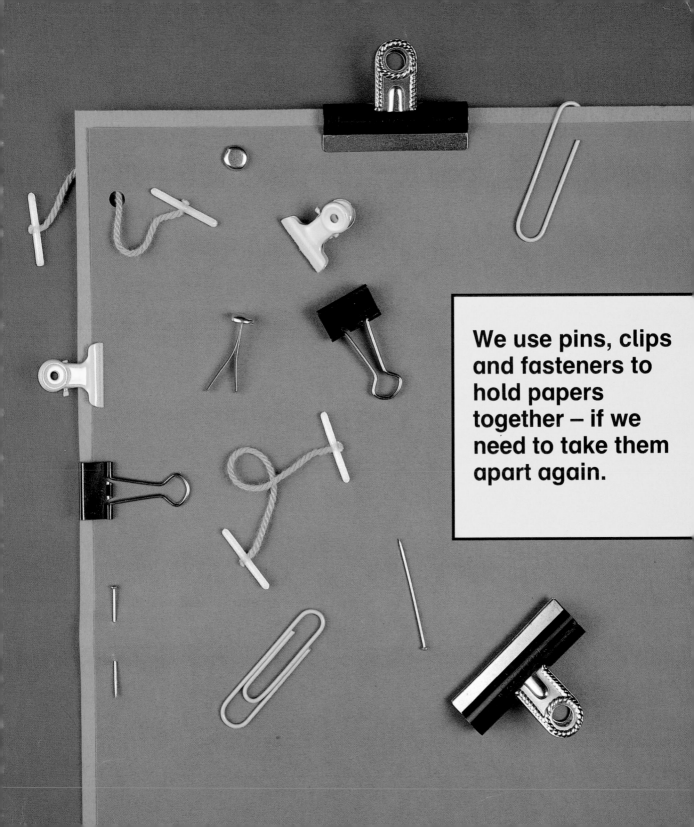

We use pins, clips
and fasteners to
hold papers
together – if we
need to take them
apart again.

If we need to fix paper more securely, we use glue or tape.

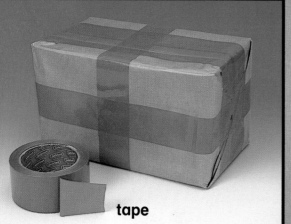

tape

glue

**What's wrong here? Why don't we join our clothes and shoes in these ways?**

These are some of the things we use for joining our clothes.
Can you think of any others?

buttons

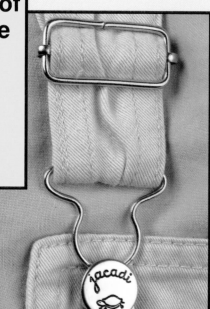

clip

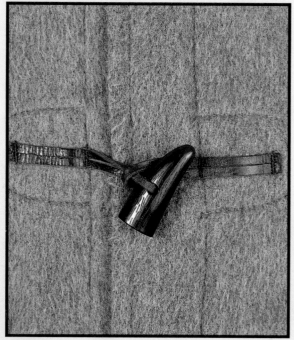

toggle

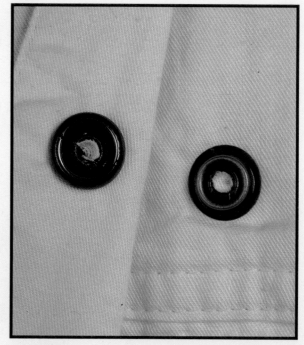

snaps

**ribbon**

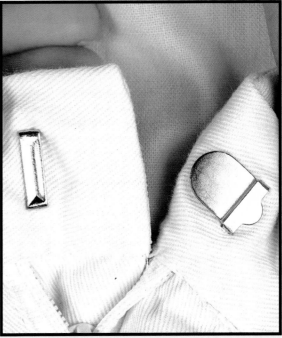

**hook and eye**

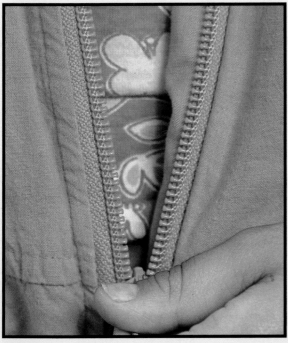

**zipper**

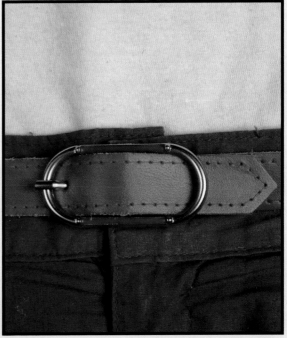

**buckle**

We can sew
a patch on
our clothes, but
we can't sew
pieces of metal.
We bolt them
instead.

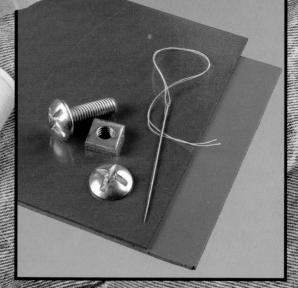

**Ribbon can be used to tie up a parcel but we would not use it to fix a broken plate!**

Some things are made with two parts that fit into each other.

We could not use a watch buckle for a coat belt, or a coat buckle for a watch strap.

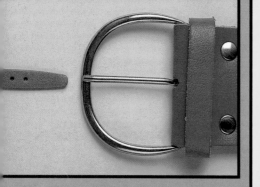

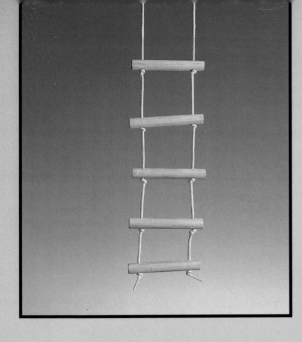

We would not use
rope for shoelaces
or use laces to
make a rope
ladder.

**Buildings are made of many different things which need to be joined together – bricks, tiles, slates, wood, metal.**

Bricks with mortar

roof tiles with nails

plastic tiles with glue

**Each kind of fastener does a particular job. We use hinges and locks on doors. We use catches on windows.**

hinge

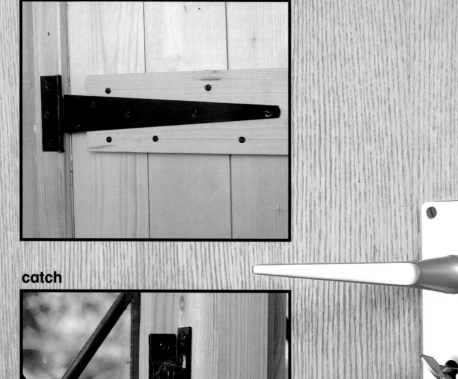

catch

lock

**bolt**

**padlock**

**hook and eye**

**safety chain**

There are many kinds of fasteners for keeping a door closed. Can you find any others in your home?

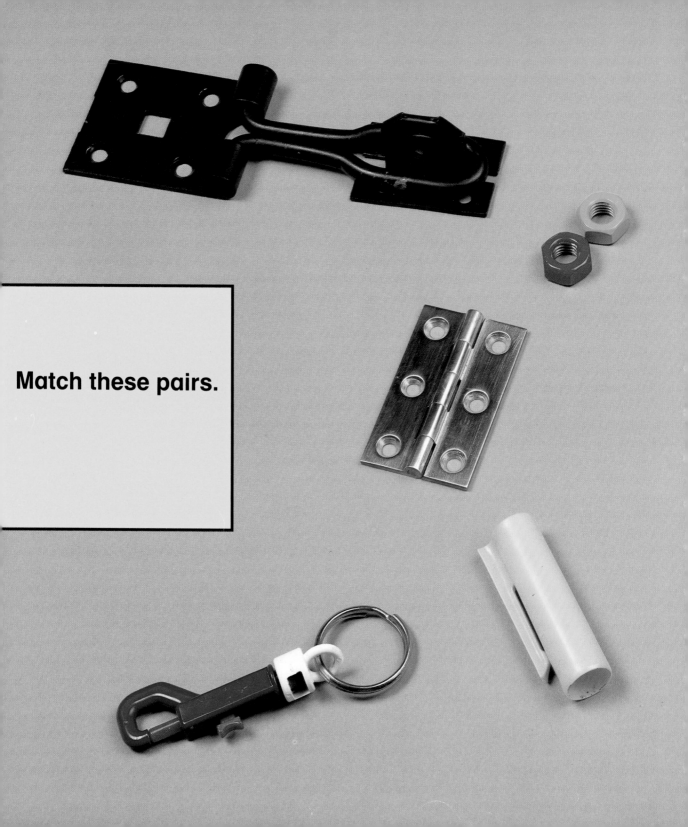

**Match these pairs.**

There are many other ways of joining things. Look around you for more.

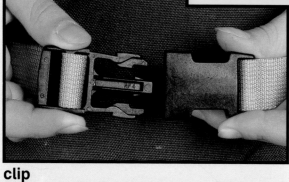

clip

safety pin

screw top

sucker

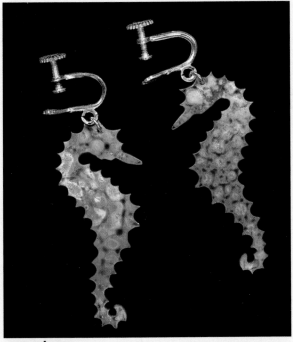

**ear-rings**

**staples**

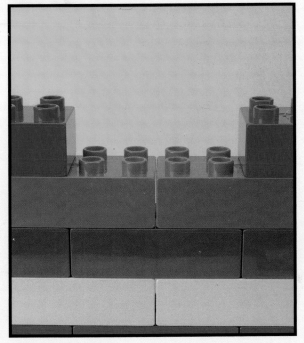

**plastic bricks**

**clasp**

# Some things to do

● Make six paper strips 6in long and 1in wide. By folding only the ends of the strips, try to join them to make one long piece.

Repeat this, using:
- Dressmaker's pins
- Paper clips
- Paste
- Scotch tape

Now you have five long paper strips, try to invent a test to decide which method of joining is the strongest.

● Brush some glue on to a square of colored card to make a pattern. Sprinkle fine sand all over the card, and then gently tap off any loose bits.

Your sand pattern follows the lines of the glue.

Make glue and sand pictures of a car, a house, a face and a person.

● Look around the room you are in. How many different ways can you find to keep things open or closed?

● Find as many things as you can which you can use to join strips of fabric together.
   Could you join two pieces of fabric together without using pins, needles, clips, glue or tape?

● Find a tube of cardboard (a paper towel center would be fine). Make two thick rolls of newspaper. Can you invent a way of using the cardboard tube to join the two rolls without using glue or tape? What must you do to get a firm joint?

## Words about joining

| | | |
|---|---|---|
| attach | hammer | sew |
| belt | hook | solder |
| bind | lace | staple |
| bolt | link | stick |
| buckle | nail | stitch |
| button | paste | tack |
| clip together | peg | tie |
| connect | pin | weld |
| couple | plug in | zip |
| fasten | push together | |
| fold together | put together | |
| fix | rivet | |
| glue | screw | |

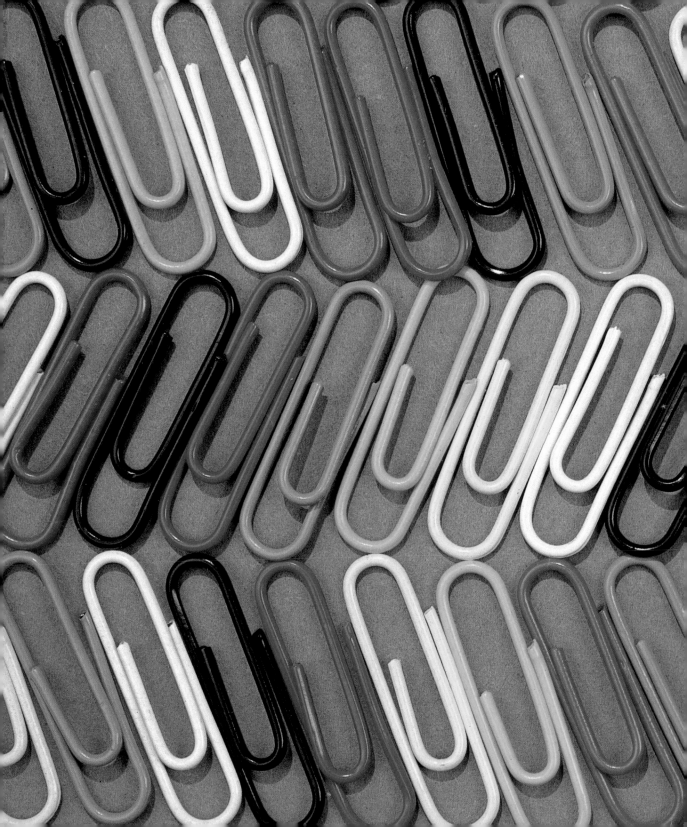

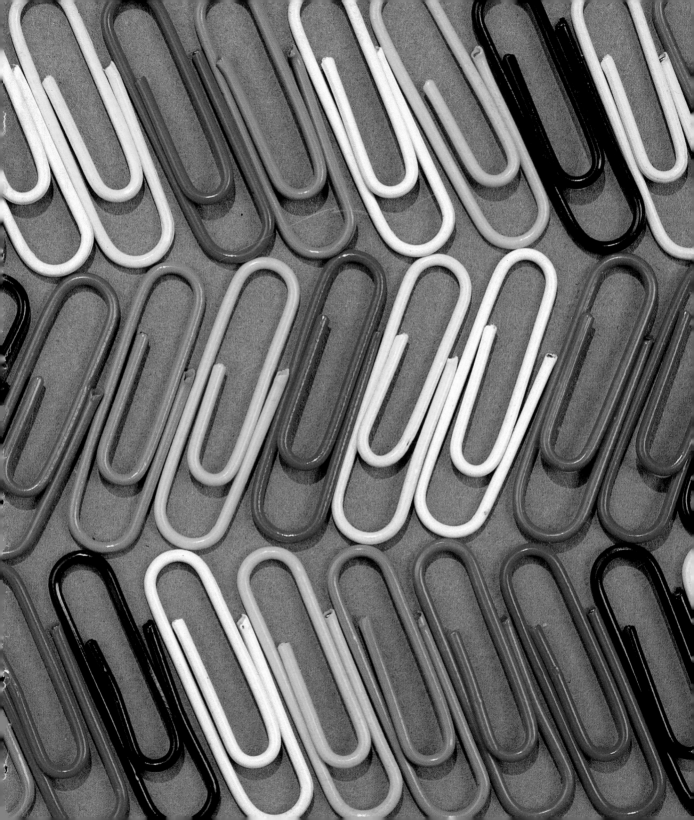